The Pendle Witch Trials of 1612

by David Holding

First published by
Scott Martin Productions, 2019
www.scottmartinproductions.com

The Expanse of Pendle Hill

First published in Great Britain in 2019 by
Scott Martin Productions
10 Chester Place,
Adlington, Chorley, PR6 9RP
scottmartinproductions@gmail.com
www.scottmartinproductions.com

Electronic version and paperback versions available for purchase on Amazon.
Copyright (c) David Holding and Scott Martin Productions

All rights reserved. Without limiting the rights under copyright reserved above, no part of this publication may be reproduced, stored or introduced into a retrieval system, or transmitted, in any form or by any means (electronic, mechanical, photocopying, recording or otherwise), without the prior written permission of both the copyright owner and the publisher of this book. No paragraph of this publication may be reproduced, copied or transmitted save with written permission or in accordance with the provisions of the Copyright Act 1956 (as amended).

ACKNOWLEDGEMENTS

It is always difficult to remember when undertaking research of any kind, all the people who helped along the way with their advice, encouragement and information. I wish to express my sincere thanks to those who played an active role in the preparation of this work, which has provided the impetus to bring about its final completion. To all these people I express my appreciation. Thanks are also due to those anonymous but ever helpful staff at the various institutions I have consulted. In particular, I would like to express my appreciation to the following:

Lancashire County Record Office, Preston.
The Harris Library, Preston.
John Rylands University of Manchester Library.
Chetham's Library and Society, Manchester.

Acknowledgement is also paid to members of the two branches of the legal profession, for the benefit of their expertise and opinions on the various issues raised in this work. My gratitude loses no sincerity in its generality. I would, however, hasten to add, that none of the above are responsible for the contents of this work, any mistakes are entirely my own.

David Holding 2019

David Holding

INTRODUCTION

Publications on the subject of witchcraft in general and the Lancashire witches in particular, continue to be a source of great interest to both young and old alike - whether as general readers or historical researchers. The impetus responsible for generating this interest came in 1848 with the publication of "The Lancashire Witches" by William Harrison Ainsworth. This book remained a major work in its field until 1951 when the equally popular novel "Mist over Pendle" by Robert Neill first appeared. Since this time, numerous publications have appeared covering the various aspects of Lancashire witchcraft. It is of particular significance that practically all these works make reference, either directly or indirectly, to what has been justly described as the 'definitive' work on the subject, namely the "Discovery of Witches" by Thomas Potts. To give the book its precise title, *"The Wonderfull Discoverie of Witches in the Countie of Lancaster",* which was first published in book form in 1613. Thomas Potts was Clerk to the Judges of Assize at Lancaster in 1612, and his book is a *verbatim* compilation of the detailed transcripts of the Trials at Lancaster in that year. As a result of the amicable collaboration of the President of the Chetham Society, James Crossley, and William Harrison Ainsworth, a copy of Pott's original book was produced in 1845 as volume six of the Society's transactions for that year.

Since 1845, no serious attempt has been made to reproduce Pott's account of the Trial in a format which will be both informative, accurate and appeal to both the general reader and local historian who may not have access to the original text. This present work is an attempt to preserve the original intention of the author in providing an accurate account of the proceedings at Lancaster in 1612, as recorded by Potts, arranged so as to carefully reflect the order of events; the preliminary examinations before the local Justice of the Peace, the taking of witness statements and gathering of evidence, culminating in the Trials at Lancaster Assize Court. Having been presented with the available evidence, it is hoped that readers will be better enabled to draw their own conclusions regarding the case for the prosecution. As a small tribute and acknowledgement to this monumental work achieved by Thomas Potts, and to the fruitful Crossley/Ainsworth partnership, I conclude this introduction with an extract from the Introduction to the 1845 publication:

> " Master Potts is a faithful and accurate chronicler and we owe his memory somewhat, for furnishing us with so elaborate a report of what took place at this time, and giving details of the various examinations of the witnesses, which contains much which throws light on the manners and language of the time, and nearly all that is necessary to enable us to form a judgement of the Trial."

THE WONDERFVLL DISCOVERIE OF WITCHES IN THE COVN-TIE OF LAN-CASTER.

With the Arraignement and Triall of Nineteene notorious WITCHES, at the Affizes and generall Gaole deliuerie, holden at the Caftle of LANCASTER, vpon *Munday, the feuenteenth of Auguft laft,*
1612.

Before Sir IAMES ALTHAM, and Sir EDWARD BROMLEY, Knights; BARONS of his Maiefties Court of EXCHEQVER: And Iuftices of *Afsize*, Oyer *and* Terminor, *and generall* Gaole deliuerie in the circuit of the *North Parts.*

Together with the Arraignement and Triall of IENNET PRESTON, at the *Afsizes holden at the Caftle of Yorke, the feuen and twentieth day of Iulie laft paft,* with her Execution for the murther of Mafter LISTER by *Witchcraft.*

Publifhed and fet forth by commandement of his Maiefties Iuftices of Affize in the North Parts.

By THOMAS POTTS *Efquier.*

LONDON,
Printed by *W. Stansby* for *John Barnes,* dwelling neare Holborne Conduit. 1613.

Source: Chetham Society Transactions Volume Six 1845.

Chapter One

Legal Background of the Period

The Role of Justices of the Peace

A Proclamation of 1195 required the appointment of Knights to 'keep the peace', and during the 13th century knights were in fact appointed solely for that purpose. Custodians of the Peace (*Custodes Pacis*) were appointed by Simon de Montfort in 1285 and continued thereafter. They were directed to receive presentments of breaches of the peace made by the constables. A Statute of 1327 (1 Edward 111. s.2. C 16) made special provision for the appointment in each county of Conservators of the Peace, who later became known as 'Justices of the Peace'. Their judicial function may be said to date from 1328 when by Statute (11 Edward 111.c.6.) they were given powers to punish offenders. By the Statute of 1345, they were empowered to hear and determine (*Oyer and Terminor*) felonies and trespasses against the peace and, by 1361 (34 Edward 111) a special Commission was assigned to each county which was to include one lord, three to four of 'the most worthy in the county', together with some person 'learned in the law'.

The Commission was finally settled by 1590 and under it, most offences could be inquired into, with a proviso that difficult cases should be reserved for the Assizes. As well as these Courts exercising judicial powers, the Justice were also responsible for the apprehension of criminals by the issue of warrants for their arrest. In the 17th century, the doubt was expressed as to whether a warrant issued without a presentment or indictment was legal, where it was directed against a person on a charge of felony. However, Sir Matthew Hale, Chief Justice of the King's Bench, and author of *Pleas of the Crown* defended its legality.

Criminal Procedure

Justices were entrusted with the preliminary examination of apprehended criminals and at first, these investigations were inquisitorial rather than judicial, the object being to acquire sufficient evidence to obtain a conviction. This preliminary examination of the facts by lay magistrates had been conducted since 1555, becoming first an agency of investigation, and later a brake on groundless indictments. The compulsory attendance of witnesses was first assigned by Statute of 1553, which gave power at the preliminary examination to bind a witness to testify at the trial. The right of the accused to be released on bail pending a final decision on the case had always existed in some form, but it was regulated by Statute from time to time, making it unavailable for many crimes - in particular witchcraft.

Trial by jury was generally regarded as the right of all persons accused of serious crimes, and from this developed rules of evidence, so designed to avoid prejudicing the minds of the lay jurors. The passing of the Witchcraft Act in 1604 increased penalties against witches - and under it, a great many witches were condemned and executed. This Act was by far the most severe, being preceded firstly by the Act of 1563 which provided the death penalty for murder by witchcraft or on a second conviction of causing bodily injury. The Act of 1542 made witchcraft a criminal offence.

The Witchcraft Act of 1604

"Be it enacted by the King's most Excellent Majesty, by and with the advice and consent of the Lords Spiritual and Temporal, and

Commons in Parliament assembled, and by the authority of the same, as follows:

That if any person or persons shall use, practise or exercise any invocation, or conjuration, of any evil and wicked spirit, or shall consult, covenant with, entertain, employ or purpose or reward any evil or wicked spirit to or for any intent or purpose or, take up any dead man, woman or child out of his, her or their grave, or any other place where the dead body resteth, or the skin, bone or any other part of any dead person, to be employed or used in any manner of witchcraft, sorcery, charm or enchantment, or shall use, practice or exercise any witchcraft, enchantment, charm or sorcery, whereby any person shall be killed, destroyed, wasted or consumed, pined or lamed in his or her body or any part thereof, every such offender or offenders, their aides, abettors and councillors being of any of the said offences duly and lawfully convicted, shall suffer pains of death as a felon or felons, and shall lose the privilege and benefit of clergy and sanctuary."

The Rules of Evidence were set aside in accusations of practising witchcraft, and we see 'hearsay' evidence being freely admitted together with widespread use being made of 'voluntary' confessions to secure convictions. To this end, unsupported and often incredulous confessions were admitted as was the uncorroborated evidence of children. It is said that during the period from 1604 to 1614, the total number of accusations of witchcraft rose higher than at any other time. The basic historical division of crimes were felonies and misdemeanours, the first depicting heinous and despicable crimes. It naturally followed from this that the felon was disloyal to the Crown and thus punishment of death was the only sentence for a felony. Misdemeanours were generally known as trespasses or transgressions, not capital offences. The punishment for these was usually by fines or imprisonment.

The procedure by which accused persons were brought to trial commenced with a complaint being lodged with the local Justice of the Peace, either verbally or by means of a Deposition (a sworn statement of fact implicating some person). The Justice would carry out an Inquiry into the complaint, taking statements from the accused and witnesses and, if there was sufficient evidence, and the crime was serious enough, the accused would be committed to the Assizes. Trials were in open court with each prisoner being Arraigned at the Bar of the Court and the Indictment being read out. The accused would be asked to plead 'Guilty' or 'Not Guilty', the jury would be sworn in and the trial would commence.

The Witch Trials of 1612 differed from present-day Criminal Court Procedure in a number of significant respects. The accused was given no opportunity to prepare any defence to the charges or to be legally represented. The accused did not know the exact nature of the charges made against him or her in advance of the trial. 'Hearsay' or uncorroborated evidence was freely admitted without production of any corroborative evidence. The most dangerous element of all, confessions, were always to be regarded as outright proof of guilt, without regard to the means by which they were obtained.

From W.H. Ainsworth's
"The Lancashire Witches"

"Beat the water, Demdike's daughter,
Till the tempest gather o'er us,
Till the thunder strikes with wonder,
And the lightenings flash before us,
Beat the water, Demdike's daughter,
Ruin seize our foe, and slaughter."

Pendle Hill (Public Attribution Photo).

David Holding

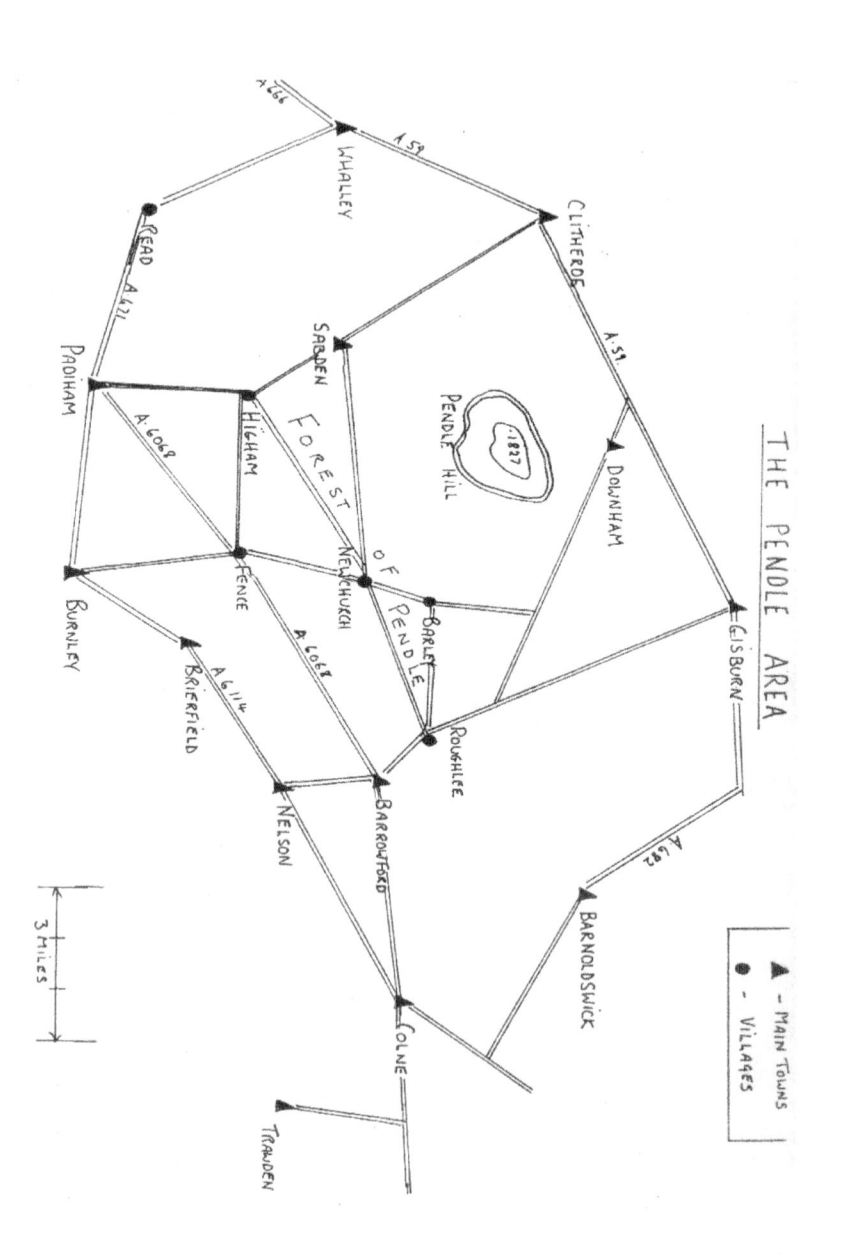

Chapter Two

The Pendle Witches and their Alleged Crimes

Living within the shadow of Pendle Hill were two rival witch families, named Demdike and Chattox. They, together with their children, struck fear into the hearts of many God-fearing people living in the Pendle Forest area of Lancashire in the early 17th century. These families claimed to possess magical powers, and nobody was prepared to put their claims to the test. The two families were essentially 'matriarchal' in organisation, in so much as they were both led by old women, their husbands having died.

Demdike, alias Elizabeth Southerns, lived with her son, He was referred to as Christopher Holgate, and was possibly from a previous marriage or illegitimate. Elizabeth also lived with a daughter widowed with three children - James, Alizon and Jennet Device (pronounced Davies). Demdike was about 80 years of age, infirm and virtually blind, so that she had to be led about by Alizon.

The rival family was led by Anne Whittle alias Chattox, who locals claimed had the most power - and was feared even by the Demdike family themselves. Chattox was also widowed and lived with daughters Elizabeth and Anne Redfearn (and Anne's husband). This bitter rivalry between the two 'witch' families could be traced back to an occasion when the home of the Demdikes, Malkin Tower, was broken into and clothing and an amount of oatmeal was stolen.

A short time later, Alizon Device saw Elizabeth Whittle wearing what she recognised as property stolen from the family home, and she promptly informed the other members of the family. John Redfearn, Anne's husband, perhaps out of a genuine fear of the power of the Demdike family, settled to pay them a year's supply of oatmeal if they would not work any harm against the Chattoxes. This was grudgingly agreed to and, for a few years, the supply was paid until one particular year, when the family failed to meet its promise. Soon afterwards, John Redfearn fell ill and died, accusing Demdike of having bewitched him. Around Christmas time in 1598, a Christopher Nutter, landowner of nearby Greenhead Farm in the Pendle Forest, had been to Burnley with his sons Robert and John, and was returning home. Robert was taken ill and, having no logical explanation for his sudden illness, blamed it on the Chattox family and Anne Redfearn in particular, because they lived on land owned by the Nutters. It appears than on one occasion, Robert Nutter had made several advances towards Anne Redfearn which she had promptly rejected, so he had decided to get his revenge by evicting the Chattox family from their home. Before this could be effected, Robert had to leave home and visit Cheshire, and it was here that he fell ill again and died shortly afterwards.

Some ten or twelve years later, Elizabeth Device had undertaken some work for a local corn-miller Richard Baldwin of Wheathead, and she considered that she had not received a fair wage for the work done. She decided to send her mother, Old Demdike to plead for her wage. Demdike, in company with young Alizon, arrived at the Baldwin house only to be met by an irate Baldwin who ordered them off his land, accusing them of being 'whores and witches'. Demdike is reputed to have muttered, "I care not for thee", which may have been regarded as a kind of curse. Some time later, Baldwin's daughter fell ill and later died. These accounts passed into folklore in the area but, more important, they helped to increase the fear of the locals and thus enhance the 'prestige' of the two rival witch families.

On Monday 18th March, 1612, Alizon Device had been out begging in the area around the township of Colne and was making her way back towards Pendle Forest. She came across an old pedlar, John Law from Halifax, whose work selling everyday items, took him around the outlying districts. Alizon asked him for some pins but she was refused. Whether the pedlar was suspicious of the request, knowing the association of clay and wax figures with pins to witchcraft will never be known. Soon after she had left him, he appears to have collapsed by the roadside and was carried to a local inn, from where a letter was despatched to his son Abraham, requesting him to see his father. He did arrive as soon as the letter had been received.

On hearing his father's account of the happening, Abraham went in search of the person responsible, Alizon Device. Having found her, she came back to the old pedlar's bedside and he charged her with bewitching him. Alizon appears to have confessed to the accusations and asked for forgiveness but, notwithstanding, she and her mother Elizabeth and brother James were brought before the local Justice of the Peace, Roger Nowell of Read Hall. Again, Alizon confessed to Nowell that she had lamed the pedlar Law through the intervention of a black dog or 'familiar'. Her information did not end there but instead, Alizon proceeded to give a vivid account of her family's dealings in witchcraft.

She made further incriminating statements regarding the rival Chattox family in deeds of witchcraft, recalling how Chattox had some disagreement with a man from the village of Higham. One John Moore had argued that Chattox had turned some of his ale sour and, in revenge, Chattox had brought about the death of Moore's son. She further claimed to have seen Chattox making clay images of the child. As a result of the careful recording of Alizon's statement, Nowell detained her, and satisfied that she was guilty on her own admissions, the other members of the family were released.

At this particular time, torture was not allowed under English law and it is unlikely that Nowell would have ignored this point. It is more likely that he would have used some form of promise of leniency in return for confirmation of the facts.

As a direct result of Alizon Device's information, Demdike, Chattox and Anne Redfearn were ordered to attend an Inquiry before Nowell on April 2nd - in the small hamlet of Fence in the Forest of Pendle. When faced with these accusations from her own grand-daughter, Demdike fully confessed that everything Alizon had said was true. As a consequence of this, Nowell detained Demdike, Chattox and Anne Redfearn, and despatched them, together with Alizon to the Castle at Lancaster.

News travelled very rapidly in the rural communities of Pendle, and it wasn't long before Nowell heard that witchcraft had not been stemmed by the despatch of the group to Lancaster. On the contrary, there had been a great gathering of witches from the whole area at Malkin Tower on Good Friday, for the purpose of plotting revenge.

On the 27th April, Nowell, together with another local Justice Nicholas Bannister from Altham, ordered that James Device, Jennet Device (a young girl of nine), and her mother Elizabeth be brought for an Inquiry. After being questioned about the Good Friday meeting, the young Jennet gave the justices another explicit and damning account. She described that a number of witches, around twenty in all, had gathered at Malkin Tower, the home of the Demdikes, on the Good Friday evening, where they feasted on meat and plotted murder. She named those present at the feast as, Elizabeth Device, John and Jane Bulcock, Christopher Holgate, Katherine Hewitt and Alice Nutter of Roughlee.

The name of Alice Nutter must have made the Justices curious with surprise because by no stretch of the imagination could she be regarded as coming from the peasant classes. Quite the opposite. She was a gentlewomen and quite wealthy by the standards of the time. Unfortunately for Alice Nutter, and in her absence, Elizabeth Device confessed that she, in concert with Nutter, had bewitched one Henry Mitton after he had refused them money. It emerged from the statements taken at the time by Nowell and Bannister, that the main purpose of the Good Friday meeting had been to devise a plot to destroy Lancaster Castle and to free the witches held there. James Device, regarded as a rather feeble person in both mind and body, readily confessed to being responsible for the deaths of Anne Towneley of Carr Hall and John Duckworth of the Laund. Anne Towneley had accused him and his mother of the theft of peat for their fire. Her death had been brought about by the making of a clay image. The second victim, Duckworth, appears to have promised James an old shirt and then gone back on his promise.

Having touched Duckworth, James with the aid of his familiar, in the shape of a dog, had killed the man.

Not content with incriminating himself beyond redemption, James went on to tell Nowell how Elizabeth, his mother, killed a local man John Robinson of Barley, by using a clay image again. Recognising that he now had sufficient evidence of serious crime, Nowell detained Elizabeth and James Device. Shortly afterwards, Elizabeth and James, together with the Bulcocks and Katherine Hewitt, were despatched to Lancaster. In the meantime, Chattox and James Device had been questioned again at Lancaster by Thomas Covell, Coroner for the County. It emerged that Demdike was dying and never stood trial for her part in the alleged witchcraft plots. There is no account as to when Alice Nutter was questioned or if in fact, she ever made a statement regarding the accusations against her. There is only the account of her trial alongside the others at Lancaster.

A period of some three months elapsed between the final questioning of Chattox and James Device and the actual opening of the Assizes at Lancaster on Monday 17th August 1612. The Trials commenced in the afternoon of Tuesday 18th August and concluded the following day, with all nine accused being found guilty as charged. The executions were carried out on Thursday 20th August outside the city walls of Lancaster at a place designated for public executions.

The Pendle Witch Trials of 1612

THE MAIN PENDLE WITCH FAMILIES

DEMDIKE

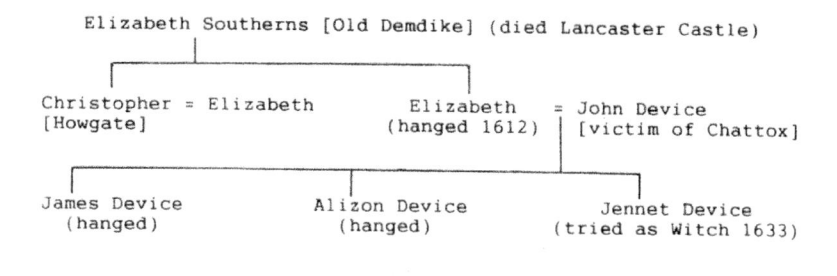

Elizabeth Southerns [Old Demdike] (died Lancaster Castle)

Christopher = Elizabeth   Elizabeth   = John Device
[Howgate]   (hanged 1612)   [victim of Chattox]

James Device   Alizon Device   Jennet Device
(hanged)   (hanged)   (tried as Witch 1633)

CHATTOX

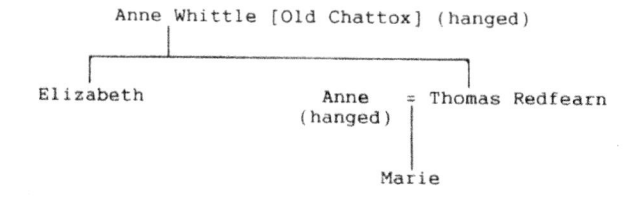

Anne Whittle [Old Chattox] (hanged)

Elizabeth   Anne   = Thomas Redfearn
                 (hanged)

Marie

NUTTERS

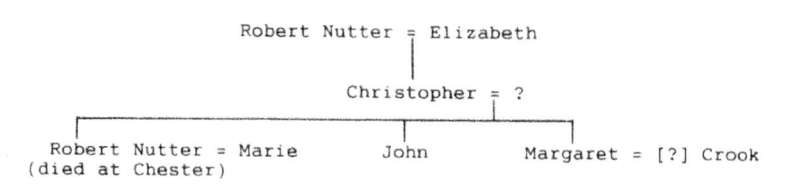

Robert Nutter = Elizabeth

Christopher = ?

Robert Nutter = Marie   John   Margaret = [?] Crook
(died at Chester)

David Holding

Chapter Three

The Trials

Gatehouse – Creative Commons Licence

     The Castle at Lancaster has been the site of an Assize Court from 1176 until 1971, when the Courts Act of that year abolished all Assizes, replacing them with Crown Courts (of which Lancaster is one). Originally Assizes were held three times a year in keeping with the Law Terms, these being January, June and October. In 1835, part of the Lancashire Assizes was transferred from Lancaster to Liverpool, and thirty years later to Manchester. As early as 1199, the site of the Castle was strengthened by adding thick walls, and in 1209 the Shire-Hall and Court were added. Henry VII is believed to have personally held court at the Castle of Lancaster, hence the legal term 'Court of the King's Bench'. Since the reign of Henry IV, all British monarchs have held the title 'Duke of Lancaster', our present Queen Elizabeth being no exception.

The Castle combined as one of H.M. Prisons until 1915 when it was used as an Internment Camp for Prisoners-of-War before returning to its role as a prison in 1954. The last Assizes was held at Lancaster Castle in 1972, and in 2011 it ceased to operate as a prison though is still in use as a Crown Court. To the north of the main gateway lies the Well Tower, with a vault on the ground floor and another deep below the surface used as a dungeon, which is reached by a long flight of rough steps. It was in this vault that the miserable victims accused of witchcraft were chained whilst awaiting their trials in 1612. Executions, particularly by hanging, were carried out on Lancaster Moor, the site now occupied by part of Lancaster Royal Grammar School.

Pre-Trial Events

Roger Nowell of Read Hall was the magistrate for Pendle and received a complaint from the family of John Law, a pedlar who claimed to have been injured by witchcraft. He began his investigations into the complaint which, as it progressed, began to implicate a significant number of persons within the Pendle district. The event that began Nowell's investigation occurred on the 21st March 1612. Demdike, one of the accused, had been regarded in the area as a witch for many years. On this particular day Demdike's grand-daughter Alizon Device, encountered John Law, a pedlar from Halifax and she had asked him for some pins, which Law refused. Whether she intended to buy them or whether she had no money and was begging for them is unclear. However, a short time after their encounter, Alizon saw Law fall down on the ground, then pick himself up and stumble to an inn. At first, Law did not accuse Alizon, but she appeared to be convinced of her magical powers when Law's son Abraham, took her to visit his father a few days after the incident. She is reported to have confessed and begged his forgiveness.

As a result of this complaint, Alizon Device, her mother Elizabeth, and her brother James, were all summoned to appear before the magistrate Nowell, on the 30th March 1612. On this occasion, Alizon confessed that she had sold her soul to the Devil, and that she had told the Devil to lame John Law because he had called her a thief. Her brother, James, stated that his sister had confessed to bewitching a child. For her part, Elizabeth admitted that her mother, Demdike, did have a mark on her body, which many would regard as having been inflicted by the Devil. When questioned further about Anne Whittle (alias Chattox), Elizabeth stated that she was regarded as having been involved in witchcraft around the Pendle area for many years. Alizon appears to have seen this as an opportunity for revenge.

In 1601, a member of the Chattox's family broke into Malkin Tower, home of the Devices, and stole goods worth about £1. Alizon accused Chattox of murdering four men by witchcraft, and of killing her own father, John Device, who died in 1601. There does appear to have been great animosity between these two rival families. On April 2nd, 1612, Demdike, Chattox and Chattox's daughter, Anne Redferne were again summoned to appear before Nowell. Both Demdike and Chattox were blind and over eighty years old, claimed that they had given their souls to the Devil some twenty years previously, providing Nowell with damaging confessions. Based on the evidence and these confessions, Nowell committed Demdike, Chattox, Anne Redfearne and Alizon Device to Lancaster Prison to be tried for causing harm by witchcraft., the term *maleficium* being used in the committal papers.

Rumours had been circulating around the Pendle area that a meeting had been organised by Elizabeth Device at Malkin Tower (the home of the Demdikes) to be held on Good Friday 10th April, 1612. When word of this meeting reached Nowell he decided to investigate. On 27th April 1612, an inquiry was held before Nowell and another magistrate, Nicholas Bannister to determine the purpose of this meeting at Malkin Tower, who had attended and what had taken place. As a direct result of this inquiry, eight further people were accused of witchcraft and committed for trial; Elizabeth Device, James Device, Alice Nutter, Katherine Hewitt, John Bulcock, Jane Bulcock, Alice Grey and Jennet Preston.

The trial of those women accused of witchcraft took place at the Lancaster Assizes on the 18th and 19th August 1612. The prosecutor was Roger Nowell who had been responsible for collecting the statements and confessions from the accused. At the trial, nine-year-old Jennet Device was a key witness for the prosecution, a practice rarely allowed in many other criminal trials in the 17th century. Jennet identified those who had attended the meeting at Malkin Tower and also gave evidence against her mother, brother and sister. Nine of the accused; Alizon Device, Elizabeth Device, James Device, Anne Whittle, Anne Redfearn, Alice Nutter, Katherine Hewitt, John Bulcock and Jane Bulcock, were found guilty during the two-day trial and hanged on 20th August 1612. Elizabeth Southerns (alias Demdike) died while awaiting trial and Alice Grey was found not guilty.

Anne Whittle (Chattox) was accused of the murder of Robert Nutter but pleaded not guilty. However, the confession she had made to Roger Nowell was read out in court, together with evidence against her from James Robinson who had resided with the Chattox family for over 20 years. He recalled how Nutter had accused Chattox of turning his beer sour, and that she was commonly believed to be a witch. Following this, Chattox admitted her guilt.

Elizabeth Device was charged with the murders of James Robinson, John Robinson and in company with Alice Nutter and Demdike, was charged with the murder of Henry Mitton. Elizabeth Device maintained her innocence of the crime. The main witness against Device was her own daughter, Jennet - a nine-year-old girl. When she was brought into the courtroom and asked to give evidence against her mother, Elizabeth began to curse and scream at her daughter so that she was removed from the courtroom. Jennet stated that she had believed her mother to be a witch for three or four years. She also said her mother had a Spirit or familiar named Ball who appeared to her in the shape of a brown dog. She also claimed to have witnessed conversations between this Spirit Ball and her mother, during which Ball had been asked to help with the various murders.

James Device gave evidence against his mother stating that he had witnessed her making a clay figure of John Robinson, one of her victims. Elizabeth Device was found guilty.

James pleaded not guilty to the murders by witchcraft of Anne Townley and John Duckworth. He, like Chattox had made a confession before Nowell, and this was read out in open court. This, together with the evidence presented against him by his sister Jennet, was sufficient to sway the jury to return a verdict of guilty.

Anne Redfearn had been charged with the murder of Robert Nutter but was acquitted due to the evidence against her being considered unsatisfactory. However, when she faced her second trial for the murder of Robert Nutter's father, Christopher Nutter, she pleaded not guilty. Demdike's statement to Nowell accusing Anne of having made figures of the Nutter family was read out in open court. Witnesses were called to testify that Anne was a witch. She refused to admit her guilt but was found guilty.

Jane Bulcock and her son, John Bulcock, were accused and found guilty of the murder of Jennet Deane by witchcraft. They both denied having attended the Malkin Tower meeting, but Jennet Device identified Jane and John as having been present.

Alice Nutter made no statement either before or during her trial, except to enter her plea of not guilty to the charge of murdering Henry Mitton by witchcraft. The prosecution alleged that she, together with Demdike and Elizabeth Device had caused Mitton's death after he had refused to give Demdike a penny she had begged from him. The only evidence against Alice appears to have been that James Device claimed that Demdike had told him of the murder, and Jennet Device's statement indicated that Alice had been present at the meeting at Malkin Tower. She was found guilty.

Katherine Hewitt was charged and found guilty of the murder of Anne Foulds and she had attended the meeting together with Alice Grey. According to James Device's evidence, both Hewitt and Grey told the others at that meeting that they had killed a child from Colne named Anne Faulds. Jennet Device also picked out Katherine at a line-up and in consequence of this, confirmed her attendance at this meeting.

Alizon Device, whose encounter with John Law had triggered the events leading up to the trials, was charged with causing harm by witchcraft. She was the only one of the accused to be confronted in court by her alleged victim, John Law. On seeing Law in court, Alizon confessed her crime and was duly found guilty.

There is no doubt that many of the allegations made in the trials resulted from members of the Demdike and Chattox families making accusations against each other in attempts to settle outstanding scores and because they were in fierce competition with each other to secure advantages and prestige in their respective communities.

Lancaster Castle Gateway (Public Attribution Photo).

The Examination, Arraignment and Trial of Notorious Witches at the Assizes and General Gaol

Delivery Held at Lancaster on Monday the Seventeenth of August 1612

Before Sir James Altham And Sir Edward Bromley Knights, Barons of His Majesty's Court of Exchequer, and Justices of Assize, Oyer and Terminor and General Gaol Delivery in the Circuit of the Northern Parts

Table of the Events of 1612

Monday 30 March
Alizon, Elizabeth and James Device examined by magistrate, Roger Nowell, at Read. Alizon held in custody and the other two released.

Thursday 2 April
Demdike, Chattox and Anne Redfearn examined at Fence by Roger Nowell, and all three detained.

Saturday 4 April
Demdike, Chattox, Anne Redfearn and Alizon Device despatched to Lancaster.

Monday 27 April
Roger Nowell and Nicholas Bannister held Enquiry at Fence. Elizabeth, James and Jennet Device questioned and detained. Later despatched to Lancaster.

Tuesday 19 May
Chattox and James Device examined at Lancaster Castle.

Monday 17 August
Assizes opened at Lancaster Castle.

Tuesday 18 August
Witch Trials began in the afternoon. Chattox, Elizabeth and James Device all found guilty.

Wednesday 19 August
Anne Redfearn tried on second charge. Alice Nutter, Katherine Hewitt, Alizon Device and John and Jane Bulcock all found guilty.

Thursday 20 August
All nine prisoners executed.

The King Against Elizabeth Southerns [Demdike]

Indicted for the Murders by Witchcraft of Richard Baldwin's Child and Richard Assheton of Downham.

Pleaded: Guilty.
Died at Lancaster Castle before her Trial.

The King Against Anne Whittle [Chattox]

Indicted for the Murders by Witchcraft of
Robert Nutter of Greenhead.
John Device.
Anne Nutter.
John Moore of Higham.
Hugh Moore of Higham.

Pleaded: Not Guilty.

The King Against Elizabeth Device.

Indicted for the Murders by Witchcraft of
John Robinson of Barley.
James Robinson of Barley.
Henry Mitton of Roughlee.

Pleaded: Not Guilty.

The Arraignment and Trial of Elizabeth Device, Daughter of Elizabeth Southerns alias Demdike, for Witchcraft, Tuesday 18th August 1612, at the Assizes and General Gaol Delivery Held at Lancaster.

Elizabeth Device

The First Indictment

Elizabeth Device, late wife of John Device of the Forest of Pendle in the County of Lancaster was indicted for practising, using and exercising wicked and devilish arts known as Witchcrafts, Charms and Sorceries on John Robinson whereby he was killed, contrary to Common Law.

The Second Indictment

The said Elizabeth Device was the second time indicted in the same manner for the death of James Robinson by Witchcraft.

The Third Indictment

The said Elizabeth Device was for the third time with others, Alice Nutter and Elizabeth Southerns alias Demdike, and her Grand-Mother, indicted for the death of Henry Mitton. To these three separate Indictments she pleaded not guilty. Her own Confession and Examination testimony was read in open court, when she was first apprehended and committed to the Castle of Lancaster by M. Nowell and M. Bannister, two of his

Majesty's Justice of the Peace for the Pendle area of Lancashire.

The Examination and Evidence of Jennet Device, Daughter of the Said Elizabeth Device Against Elizabeth Device, her Mother, Prisoner at the Bar Upon Her Arraignment and Trial

Jennet Device, daughter of Elizabeth Device confessed that her mother was a Witch because she had seen her Spirit in her mother's house which is called Malkin Tower. The Spirit was in the form of a brown dog which she called Ball, and at one time the said Spirit asked her mother what she would wish him to do, and her mother asked for help to kill John Robinson of Barley. The Spirit told her mother that the said Robinson had been killed by witchcraft accordingly, and her mother has continued as a Witch for the over four years.

She further confessed that about a year after Robinson's death, her mother called for the Spirit Ball, who appeared asking what she wished to be done. Her mother asked the Spirit to kill James Robinson of Barley, brother to John, and Ball agreed to do it, and about three weeks later, James died. She also confessed that she was present at one time when her mother called for Ball. Ball asked her what she would have done, and her mother said she wanted him to him kill a person called Mitton of Roughlee, so Ball said he would do it. About three weeks later, the person, Mitton, died.

Jennet Device further stated that on Good Friday last year there were about twenty persons, two of them being men, at Malkin Tower at about twelve o'clock. Her mother had said that all these persons were Witches and that they had come to give a name to Alizon Device's own Spirit. She is now a prisoner in Lancaster Castle.

She identified the names of six of the witches present at this meeting. The wife of Hugh Hargreaves, Christopher Howgate her uncle, and Elizabeth his wife, the wife of Richard Miles, Christopher Kay and his wife, the names of the rest she was not certain of. Her mother and brother were both there.

The Examination and Evidence of James Device, Son of Elizabeth Device Against Elizabeth Device, His Mother, the Prisoner at the Bar Upon her Arraignment and Trial

James Device stated that on Good-Friday last year, at about twelve o'clock in the day, there were a number of persons of which three were men and the rest women, dining at Malkin Tower. They met there for three reasons his mother had told him. The first was for the naming of the Spirit of Alizon Device - his sister, the second was for the delivery of his Grand-Mother Demdike, his sister Anne Chattox and her daughter Anne Redfearn from the Castle. The third reason was for the killing of the Gaoler at Lancaster and before the next Assizes, to blow up the Castle at Lancaster. All these plans James Device had heard for himself. He also said that the names of the Witches at the Good-Friday meeting at his Grand-Mother's house and then at his own mother's were, the wife of Hugh Hargreaves, the wife of Christopher Bulcock and John her son, the mother of Miles Nutter, Elizabeth the wife of Christopher Hargreaves, Christopher Howgate and Elizabeth his wife, and Alice Gray, together with himself and his mother.

He stated that after all the Witches left the house they got on horseback and immediately vanished out of his sight. Before they parted, they all arranged to meet at the home of Preston's wife, in twelve months' time.

The King Against James Device

Indicted for the Murder by Witchcraft of Anne Towneley of Carr Hall and John Duckworth of the Laund.

Pleaded: Guilty.

Indicted on a Second Charge for the Murder by Witchcraft of John Hargreaves of Goldshawbooth, and Blaze Hargreaves of Higham.

Pleaded: Not Guilty.

The Voluntary Confession of James Device, Prisoner in The Castle at Lancaster

He heard his Grand-Mother say that his mother Elizabeth Device and others, had killed Henry Mitton of Roughlee by Witchcraft. The reason why he was killed was that his Grand-Mother had asked him for a penny and had been refused, so she procured his death. He further stated that about three years ago, when he was in his Grand-Mother's house with his mother, there came a thing in the shape of a brown dog, which his mother called Ball, who spoke to his mother and bid her make a picture of clay in the likeness of John Robinson, dry it hard, and then crumble it bit by bit, and as the picture should crumble, so should John Robinson, his body decaying and wasting away. After his mother had agreed, the dog vanished from sight. The next day, he saw his mother take some clay and make a picture out of it, to resemble that of John Robinson. She brought it into the house and dried it for two days. After it was thoroughly dried, his mother began crumbling the picture, every day a little, for some three weeks altogether. Within two days of all being crumbled away, John Robinson died.

He further stated that twelve years ago at a burial at the New Church in Pendle, Anne Chattox removed three heads of buried people from graves and drew eight teeth out of the heads, keeping four for herself and giving four to Demdike, his Grand-Mother.

The following day being Good-Friday, about twelve o'clock in the daytime, a number of people dined in his mother's house, three were men together with himself, and the rest women. His mother had told him that they were meeting for three reasons. Firstly, for the naming of the Spirit of Alizon Device, now a prisoner at Lancaster. Secondly, for the delivery of his Grand-Mother, his sister Alizon, Anne Chattox and her daughter Anne Redfearn, for the killing of the Gaoler at Lancaster, and before the next Assizes, to blow up the Castle at Lancaster, so that by these means, the witches might escape. Thirdly, for the killing of Master Lister of Westby because he had borne malice against one of the witches, and she did not have the power strong enough to do it herself.

    He gave the names of the witches who were present at the Good-Friday meeting as; the wife of Hugh Hargreaves, the wife of Christopher Bulcock and John her son, Alice Nutter, mother of Miles Nutter, Christopher Howgate and his wife, himself and his mother. James Device, Prisoner in the Castle at Lancaster said that his Spirit Dandy desperately wanted his Soul, then he would give him power to revenge himself against any whom he disliked. The Spirit appeared to him at different times in the likeness of a dog and each time earnestly tried to persuade him to give his Soul. The last time that the Spirit appeared to him, he was still refusing to give his Soul, so the Spirit gave a most fearful cry which caused a great flash of fire to surround it. After this he never saw the Spirit again.

The Examination and Evidence of Jennet Device
Against James Device, Her Brother

Jennet Device stated that on Good-Friday last, there were about twenty persons of which two were men, at her Grand-Mother's house called Malkin Tower, about twelve o'clock, all such persons her mother said were Witches. They had come to give a name to Alizon Device's Spirit or Familiar. All those present dined on beef, bacon and mutton being from the fowl stolen from Robinson's of Barley. She further said the names of six of the said Witches, the wife of Hugh Hargreaves, Christopher Howgate her uncle, Dick Mile's wife, Christopher Jacks and his wife, but the names of the rest she did not know. Her mother and brother were both there.

On being examined in open court, she said that her brother James Device, Prisoner at the Bar, had been a Witch for the past three years, about the beginning of which time there appeared to him in his mother's house, a black dog which her brother called Dandy. She further said that about twelve months ago, in her presence, her brother called for Dandy and it appeared to him and asked what it could do for him. Her brother asked Dandy to help him kill Mistress Towneley, whereupon Dandy said that her brother would have his best help to do what he wanted. Dandy said, in her hearing, that he would kill Mistress Towneley.

Being on oath, she further stated that Dandy appeared once again to her brother, asking what he would have him do, and her brother asked him to kill John Hargreaves, Dandy said that he would do it, and now John Hargreaves is dead. On another occasion, her brother called on Dandy and requested him to kill

Blaze Hargreaves, and Dandy said that he would and now Blaze Hargreaves is dead.

The King Against Anne Redfearn

Indicted with having caused the death by Witchcraft of Christopher Nutter of Greenhead.

Pleaded: Not Guilty.
Acquitted.

Indicted on a Second Charge with the Murder by Witchcraft of Robert Nutter.

Pleaded: Not Guilty.

The Arraignment and Trial of Anne Redfearn, Daughter of Anne Whittle, Alias Chattox, on Wednesday 19th August, 1612, at the Assizes and General Gaol Delivery Held at Lancaster.

Anne Redfearn was Indicted for practising Witchcrafts, Charmes and Sorceries on Christopher Nutter which killed him. She was Indicted for practising Witchcrafts, Charmes and Sorceries on Christopher Nutter whereby this brought about his death. She pleaded Not Guilty.

The Examination of Elizabeth Southerns, Alias Demdike, 2nd April 1612. Against Anne Redfearn, Daughter of Anne Whittle, Prisoner at the Bar.

Elizabeth Southerns stated that about six months before Robert Nutter died, she went to the house of Thomas Redfearn, and at the east end of the house, she saw Anne Whittle and Anne Redfearn with two pictures of clay lying by the side of them, with a third picture being made by Anne Whittle. Anne Redfearn brought her mother some clay to complete the third picture. The Spirit, Tibb, in the shape of a black cat, appeared to her. Elizabeth Southerns asked the Spirit what they were doing. The Spirit told her they were making three pictures, then she asked whose pictures they were. The Spirit said that they were the pictures of Christopher Nutter, Robert Nutter and Mary his wife.

The Examination of John Nutter of Higham Booth, in the Forest of Pendle, in the County of Lancaster Yeoman, Against Anne Redfearn

John Nutter stated on oath said that about Christmas some eighteen or nineteen years ago, when he was coming from Burnley with Christopher Nutter and Robert Nutter - his father and brother, he heard his brother say to his father that he was sure that he had been bewitched by the Chattox family members, Anne Chattox and Anne Redfearn. He pleaded with his father to have them taken to Lancaster Castle. His father did not take this accusation seriously but said that the cause of his illness was his own doing. He swore that if he returned from his duties for Sir Richard Shuttleworth, he would see them taken away.

The Examination of James Device Against Anne Redfearn

James Device stated that about two years ago, he saw three pictures of clay at the end of Redfearn's house, and that Anne Redfearn had one of the pictures in her hand and was crumbling it. He could not tell whose pictures they were.

The King Against Alice Nutter

Indicted for the Murder by Witchcraft of Henry Mitton of Roughlee, in concert with Elizabeth Southerns alias Demdike, and Elizabeth Device.

Pleaded: Not Guilty.

The Examination of James Device, Son of Elizabeth Device, Taken the 7th April 1612 Before Roger Nowell and Nicholas Bannister, Two of his Majesty's Justices of the Peace in The County of Lancaster Against Alice Nutter.

James Device stated on oath that he heard his Grand-Mother say that his mother, Elizabeth Device and his said Grand-Mother and Alice Nutter, the wife of Richard Nutter, had killed one Henry Mitton of Roughlee by Witchcraft.

The reason why he was killed was that his Grand-Mother had asked Henry Mitton for a penny, and that he had refused her, so she procured his death. Upon Good Friday at about twelve o'clock in the day time, there dined at his mother's house a number of persons, three of whom were men including himself, and the rest women, and they met for three reasons, so his mother had told him. The first was for the naming of the Spirit of Alizon Device who could not name him, being prisoner at Lancaster. The second reason was for the delivery of his Grand-Mother, his sister Alizon, Anne Chattox and her daughter Anne Redfearn.

The third reason was for the killing of the Gaoler at Lancaster before the next Assizes, to blow up the Castle at Lancaster so by that means, they could make good their escape. The names of the witches who were at his Grand-Mother's house on Good Friday and now his own mother's house, were so many, but he did know that among them was Alice Nutter, mother of Miles Nutter. He also stated that all the witches went out of the house and got onto horses, some of one colour and some of another; they then all vanished out of his sight. Before they finally parted, they all arranged to meet at Preston's wife's house the same day in twelve months, at which occasion she, Preston's wife would make a great feast for them.

The Examination and Evidence of Jennet Device Daughter of Elizabeth Device Against Alice Nutter, Prisoner at the Bar.

Jennet Device said that on Good Friday last, there were about twenty persons, of which two were men, at her Grand-Mother's house at Malkin Tower about twelve o'clock, all of which her mother said were Witches. She also said that she knew the names of six of them; the wife of Hugh Hargreaves, Christopher Howgate, her uncle, and Elizabeth his wife, Dick Mile's wife, Christopher Jacks and his wife - but that the names of the rest she did not know. After these examinations were openly completed, his Lordship being very suspicious of this young girl, Jennet Device, and ordered her to be taken into the Upper Hall, to test her evidence. Master Covell, Gaoler at Lancaster, was ordered to set all his prisoners in a line, and between every suspected Witch, place another prisoner and also some other women, so that no child could tell the one from the other.

Jennet Device was ordered to be brought into Court and she was examined again by his Lordship on every point of her evidence. What women were at Malkin Tower on Good-Friday? How she knew them? What were the names of any of them? In the end, his Lordship asked whether she knew any of them lined up and she told them she could. In the presence of this great audience, and in open court, she went and took Alice Nutter, the Prisoner, by the hand and accused her to be a Witch, and told her in what place she sat at the feast at Malkin Tower, at the great assembly of Witches, and who sat next to her, what conference they had and the rest of the proceedings - all without any contradiction.

The King Against Katherine Hewitt

Indicted for the Murder by Witchcraft of Anne Foulds of Colne.

Pleaded: Not Guilty.

The Arraignment and Trial of Katherine Hewitt of Colne, in The County of Lancaster, for Witchcraft, on Wednesday 19th August 1612, at the Assizes and General Gaol Delivery Held at Lancaster

Katherine Hewitt, Prisoner in the Castle at Lancaster, was Indicted for practising and exercising Witchcrafts, and Sorceries on Anne Foulds thereby causing her death. She pleaded Not Guilty.

The Examination of James Device, Son of Elizabeth Device, Taken the 27th April 1612 Before Roger Nowell and Nicholas Bannister, Two of His Majesty's Justices of The Peace in the County of Lancaster Against Katherine Hewitt of Colne

Elizabeth Device confessed, stating that on Good Friday last, there dined at her house what she knew to be Witches, amongst them was Katherine Hewitt. At that meeting on Good Friday at Malkin Tower, Katherine Hewitt and one Anne Gray confessed that they had killed a child of Fould's called Anne Foulds. She also stated that Katherine Hewitt together with all present, gave her consent with Pearson's wife, for the murder of Master Lister.

The Examination and Evidence of Jennet Device Against Katherine Hewitt, Prisoner at the Bar.

Jennet Device said that on Good Friday last, at about twelve o'clock, there were about twenty persons, two of them men, at her Grand-Mother's house called Malkin Tower. All these persons her mother told her were Witches, and she knew the names of six of the said Witches. She was then commanded by his Lordship to find and point out the said Katherine Hewitt from amongst all the rest of the women. She went and took the said Katherine Hewitt by the hand, accused her to be one and told her in what place she sat at the feast at Malkin Tower.

The King Against John Bulcock and Jane Bulcock

Indicted for having feloniously practised Witchcraft on the body of Jennet Deane of Newfield Edge, so that she was consumed and finally went mad.
Pleaded: Not Guilty.

The Arraignment and Trial of John Bulcock and Jane Bulcock His Mother, of the Moss End in The County of Lancaster, For Witchcraft on Wednesday 19th August 1612, at the Assizes and General Gaol Delivery Held at Lancaster

John Bulcock and Jane Bulcock, his mother, were Indicted for practising and using Witchcraft upon the body of Jennet Deanet so that she became mad.
They pleaded Not Guilty.

The Examination of James Device Taken the 27th Day of April 1612, Before Roger Nowell and Nicholas Bannister, Two of His Majesty's Justices of The Peace in the County of Lancaster Against John and Jane Bulcock

James Device stated that on Good Friday about twelve o' clock in the daytime, there dined at his mother's house a number of persons of which three were men together with himself, and the rest were women. According to his mother, they had met for three reasons. The first was for the naming of the Spirit of Alizon Device, now Prisoner at Lancaster. The second was for the delivery of his Grand-Mother, his sister Alizon, Anne Chattox and her daughter Anne Redfearn. The third was for the killing of the Gaoler at Lancaster and, for the blowing up of the Castle before the next Assizes so that they could make good their escape.
He further stated that the names of the Witches who were present at the Good Friday meeting were Jane Bulcock and John Bulcock her son - amongst others. He said that all the Witches went out of the

house and once outside they got on horseback. Preston's wife was the last to leave, and once on horseback, they all vanished out of his sight. He further said that John Bulcock, and Jane his mother, confessed on Good Friday at Malkin Tower in his hearing, that they had bewitched a woman the wife of John Deane, but he did not hear them give the woman's name. He further stated that at the feast at Malkin Tower, he heard them all give their consent to the killing of Master Thomas Lister of Westby by Witchcraft. After the death of Master Lister, they all agreed and gave consent to the death of one Leonard Lister.

The Examination of Elizabeth Device, Taken 21st April 1612, Against John Bulcock and Jane Bulcock His Mother

Elizabeth Device stated on oath that she truly thought that the Bulcocks know the names of some of the Witches who lived around the area of Padiham and Burnley. She further stated that, at the meeting at Malkin Tower, Katherine Hewitt and John Bulcock, together with the rest that were present, gave their consents to the killing of Master Lister.

The Examination and Evidence of Jennet Device Against John Bulcock and Jane, His Mother,
Prisoners at the Bar

Jennet Device said that on Good Friday last, there were about twenty persons, two of which were men, at her Grand-Mother's house called Malkin Tower.

All of these persons, according to her mother, were Witches and she knew the names of six of them. Jennet Device was then commanded by His Lordship to find and point out the said John Bulcock and Jane Bulcock from the rest. She went and took Jane Bulcock by the hand and accused her to be a Witch. She further accused John Bulcock.

The King Against Alizon Device

Indicted with having caused grievous harm by Witchcraft to John Law of Halifax.

Pleaded: Guilty.

The Arraignment and Trial of Alizon Device, Daughter of Elizabeth Device, Within the Forest of Pendle in the County of Lancaster, For Witchcraft

Alizon Device was Indicted for practising and exercising Witchcrafts, Charms and Sorceries on John Law whereby he was lamed.

The Confession of Alizon Device, Prisoner At the Bar, Published and Declared at the Time of Her Arraignment and Trial in Open Court

She stated that about two years ago, her Grand-Mother called Elizabeth Southerns alias Demdike, on many of the occasions whilst they were out begging together, persuaded and advised her to let a Devil or Familiar appear to her and let it suck at some part of her. She may then have anything she wished for, or else any act she wished to be carried out by the Spirit. Not long afterwards, while she was walking towards Roughlee, in a close of John Robinson's there appeared to her a thing like a black dog which spoke to her desiring her to give it her Soul. Being enticed to agreeing, the black dog sucked at her breast and the place remained blue for over six months. The dog did not appear again until the eighteenth day of March last year at which time she met with a pedlar on the highway near Colne. She demanded from the pedlar some pins, but he refused to untie his pack. As she left him, the black dog appeared to her and asked her what she would have him do to the man. She asked what he could do at him, whereupon the dog replied that it could lame him. She then replied, "Lame him".

Before the pedlar had gone far, he fell down lame and was carried away into a nearby house and laid down. She went on her way begging in Trawden Forest all day and came home at night. About five days later, the black dog appeared again as she was going begging in a close near the Newchurch in Pendle, and it requested that she stay and speak with it, but she refused. Since that time, it had never appeared again to her.

The Evidence of John Law, Petty-Chapman On His Oath Against Alizon Device, Prisoner At the Bar

He stated that about the eighteenth of March last year, he being a pedlar, went with his pack of wares on his back through Colnefield, where unluckily he met with Alizon Device. She was very earnest with him for pins, but he could not give her any, and she appeared very angry with him. When he was past her, he fell down lame and managed to get into an alehouse in Colne. He lay there in great pain and was unable to move either his hands or feet, and he saw a great black dog stand by him. It had very fearful fiery eyes, great teeth and a very fierce face, and it made him very frightened. Immediately afterwards, Alizon Device came in and looked at him before leaving. Afterwards he was tormented both day and night with Alizon Device and continues being lame and unable to travel.

With weeping tears, he turned to Alizon Device, and speaking so that all in court could hear him said: "You know this to be true".

Alizon Device acknowledged this to be true and prayed that the victim would forgive her offence, which he freely and voluntarily did.

The Examination of Abraham Law of Halifax, In the County of York, Clotheir, Taken Upon Oath on the 13th of March 1612, Before Roger Nowell, Justice of the Peace for the County of Lancaster

Being sworn, he stated that on Saturday last, being the twenty first of March, he was sent for by a letter from his father, that he should come to him who lay in Colne, lame. When he came to his father, he had recovered his speech and he complained about the pain he was having. He said that his illness had been done to him at Colnefield soon after Alizon Device had asked for some pins from him, and that his lameness was done by Witchcraft. Seeing his father so tormented with the said Alizon, he went in search of her and having found her, brought her back to his father. His father, in his own hearing and others present, charged the said Alizon with having bewitched him, which confessing, the said Alizon asked her father to forgive him, which he accordingly did.

It was affirmed to the Court that John Law the pedlar, before his unfortunate meeting with this Witch, was a very able and stout man of body and of goodly stature. By the devilish art of Witchcraft, his head is drawn, his eyes and face deformed, his speech difficult to understand, his legs lame and his left side also lame. His body is unable to endure any travel, and he remains in this condition at the present time. Alizon Device being questioned by the Court whether she could help the poor pedlar to recover his former strength and health, answered that she could not and so did many of the rest of the witches present. She, together with others, affirmed that if old Demdike had lived, she could and would have helped him out of that great misery. She acknowledged the Indictment against her to be true.

The Names of the Prisoners at the Bar to Receive Their Judgement of Life and Death:

ANNE WHITTLE alias CHATTOX.
ELIZABETH DEVICE.
JAMES DEVICE.
ANNE REDFEARN
ALICE NUTTER.
KATHERINE HEWITT.
JOHN BULCOCK.
JANE BULCOCK.
ALIZON DEVICE.

ALL FOUND GUILTY.

The Judgement of the Right Honourable Sir Edward Bromley, Knight, One of His Majesty's Justices of Assize at Lancaster, Upon the Witches Convicted as Follows: -

"There is no man alive more unwilling to pronounce this woeful and heavy Judgement against you than myself; and if it were at all possible, I would to God this cup might pass from me. But since it is otherwise provided, that after all proceedings of the Law, there must be a Judgement, and the Execution of that Judgement must succeed and follow in due time, I pray to have patience to receive that which the Law doth lay upon you. You of all people have the least cause to complain, since in the Trial of your lives, there has been great care and pains taken, and much time spent, and very few or none of you but stand now convicted upon your own voluntary confessions and Examinations. Few witnesses against you, but such as were present and parties in your Assemblies. Nay, I may further affirm, what persons of your nature and condition ever were Arraigned and Tried with more solemnity, had more liberty given to plead or answer to every particular point of Evidence against you?

In conclusion, such has been the general care of all that had to deal with you, that you have neither causes to be offended in the proceedings of the Justices, that first took pains in these matters nor with the Court that has had great care to give nothing in evidence against you but matter of fact; sufficient matter upon record, and not to induce or lead the Jury to find any of you to be guilty upon matter of suspicion, nor with the witnesses who have been tried, as it were in the fire; nay you cannot deny but must confess what extraordinary means have been used to make trial of their evidence, and to discover the least intended practice in any one of them, to touch your lives unjustly.

As you stand simply (your offences and bloody practices not considered), your fall would rather move compassion than exasperate any man. For whom would not ruin of so many poor creatures at one time, as in appearance simple and of little understanding? But the blood of those innocent children and others of His Majesty's subjects, whom cruelly and barbarously you have murdered, have cried out unto the Lord against you, and solicited for satisfaction and revenge. It is therefore now time no longer wilfully to strive both against the providence of God and the Justices of the Land; the more you labour to acquit yourselves, the more evident and apparent you make your offences to the World.

Impossible it is that they shall either prosper or continue in this World, or receive reward in the next, that are stained with so much innocent blood. The worst then I wish to you, standing at the Bar convicted, to receive your Judgement, is remorse and true repentance for the safeguarding of you Souls, and after an humble, penitent and hearty acknowledgement of your grievous sins and offences, committed both against God and Man.

First, yield humble and hearty thanks to Almighty God for His taking hold of you in your beginning, and making stay of your intended bloody practices (although God knows there is too much done already), which would in time have cast so great a weight of Judgement upon your Souls. Then praise God that it pleased him not to surprise or strike you suddenly, even in the execution of your bloody murders, and in the midst of you wicked practices, but have given you time, and takes you away by a judicial course and trial of the Law. Last of all, crave pardon of the World, and especially of all such as you have justly offended, either by tormenting them, their children or friends, murder of their kinsfolk or loss of any of their goods.

And for leaving to future times the president of so many of these barbarous and bloody murders, with such meetings, practices, consultations and means to execute revenge, being the greatest part of your comfort in all your actions, which may instruct others to hold the like course or fall in the like sort. It only remains I pronounce the Judgement of the Court against you by the King's authority which is; You shall all go from hence to the Castle, from whence you came, from there you shall be carried to the place of Execution for this County; where your bodies shall be hanged until you are dead; and God have Mercy on your Souls. For your comfort in this world, I shall commend a learned and worthy Preacher to instruct you, and prepare you for another World; All I can do for you is to pray for your repentance in this World; the satisfaction of many; and forgiveness in the next World, for saving your Souls, and God grant you may make good use of the time you have in this world, to his glory and your own comfort."

Source: Chetham Society Transactions, Volume vi 1845.

Chapter Four
A Legal Review of the Trials

The first prisoner to appear at the Bar was Anne Whittle, alias Chattox, whom Potts described as a 'dangerous witch', and but for the enormity of her crimes, her 'contrition would have moved them (the Jury) to pity'. It would appear that Roger Nowell, the local Justice of the Peace who prosecuted at the Trials, requested two statements made before him on the 2nd April 1612, to be read out in Open Court. The first statement was Chattox's own 'voluntary' confession to being a witch. The second statement made by Demdike, is the one in which she witnessed, before the death of Robert Nutter, Anne Whittle (alias Chattox) and Anne Redfearn, making clay pictures, one of which was of Robert Nutter. These two statements taken together, appear to have provided sufficient corroborative evidence for the Jury to secure the conviction of Chattox. However, Potts places particular emphasis on the fact that "a voluntary confession of a witch doth excel all other evidence".

Justices of the Peace were entrusted with the 'preliminary examination' of apprehended criminals by two statutes of Philip and Mary [1 & 2 P & M, and 2 & 3 P & M, c.10). At first these investigations were inquisitorial rather than judicial, the object being to acquire sufficient evidence to obtain a conviction through the close examination of the accused, who was not present when the witnesses for the prosecution were examined. Justices were also responsible for the apprehension of criminals by the issue of warrants for their arrest. By the statute of 5 Eliz.c9 (1562), witnesses could be compelled to attend court. This indicates that by the seventeenth century the practice of examination of witnesses had become a common legal procedure.

At the end of her trial, Chattox, realising that the cards were firmly stacked against her, acknowledged all the evidence against her to be true, thus convicting herself by her own admission. The next to appear was Elizabeth Device who, while pleading Not Guilty, had already confessed to the charges against her at her preliminary examination conducted by Justices Nowell and Bannister on 27th April 1612. Nowell produced in evidence a statement of Jennet Device, her own daughter, which implicated her in the crimes with which she was charged. This was followed by the reading, in Open Court, of part of James Device's statement or confession. At first Elizabeth denied all the accusations and retracted her original confession. Finally realising that her efforts were in vain, she acknowledged their truth.

The appearance of James Device in court today would raise issues of admissibility, regarding whether such a defendant was fit to plead, let alone stand trial. He appeared as a mentally retarded youth who was also physically weak. Notwithstanding, Potts took sufficient trouble to faithfully record written evidence to justify his standing trial and to prove his guilt. He admitted to both of the original murders with which he was charged, and his statement was read out in Open Court. It was acknowledged by him as being a true record of the facts.

At this stage in the proceedings, Nowell produced nine-year-old Jennet Device in person, to help convict her own brother.

Anne Redfearn was the next to be Arraigned at the Bar, and she maintained her innocence of all charges against her. Significantly, Potts does not record any statement made by her at any stage in the proceedings. She does appear to have been the victim of a persecution campaign, having been acquitted on one Indictment, only to be put on trial again for another. Her imputed crime was that she was accused of cursing to death a person who did not even accuse her of any crime. The identical statements which were used against her mother were again read out in Open Court, together with Demdike's account of her involvement, together with a further statement from Margaret Crook.

The only real offence implicating Anne Redfearn was her rejection of the improper advances of the young Robert Nutter, for whose death she was later indicted. She continued to protest her innocence right up to the end.

As far as Alice Nutter is concerned, it does appear that Roger Nowell, the local Justice of the Peace entered in the prosecution as a willing participant to an obvious conspiracy, arising from a grudge he nursed over a long-disputed boundary.

Alice is described by Potts as the wife of Richard Nutter of Roughlee and the mother of Miles Nutter. What emerges is the fact that Alice was the victim of a very elaborate conspiracy in which the prime movers were members of her own family. It is difficult to dismiss the suspicion that her considerable wealth was a great disadvantage to her, given that her own relatives appeared to have done very little to save her. The evidence against her was not only purely 'hearsay' but bordering on the absurd. Yet despite this, she was convicted solely on the strength of James and Elizabeth Device's statements, and the identification evidence of the child Jennet Device. She pleaded not guilty and protested her innocence to the end.

Katherine Hewitt was convicted on the strength of a statement made by James Device on the 27th April, together with a portion of Elizabeth Device's statement. Once again, Jennet's identification evidence helped to secure Katherine Hewitt's conviction.

John and Jane Bulcock were similarly convicted on the strength of James Device's statement and Jennet's intervention.

Alizon Device was the last to be tried in this sad catalogue of events, having not pleaded either way to the charges made against her when she was Arraigned. Judge Bromley required her to make an open declaration of the offence, which Potts agreed confirmed her confession made on the 30th March before Nowell - thus securing her conviction.

The victim of her alleged crime, the pedlar John Law, appeared in Court as a witness, and the statement of his son Abraham was also presented in evidence. It is very important in assessing the evidence against the defendants, to remember that many of the accusations levelled at the various members of the Pendle 'witch' community, were a means of settling old scores, and many were of such dubious foundation that they would not be taken seriously today. Yet when taken out of their real context, they formed a vital part of the prosecution's case, however exaggerated they may have been. The Trials were also held at a time when superstition was rife and played an important part of rural life in Stuart England. In the neighbourhood of Pendle, local customs were an integral part of everyday life, and things that could not be explained through the limited logic of country people, were put down to Witchcraft.

The trial of Witches in courts of law depended to a large extent on what was considered acceptable proof at a particular period in time. Hearsay evidence, the uncorroborated evidence of children, lies and malicious allegations were all accepted as evidence against a suspected witch. In the absence of such 'evidence', persuasion by means of trickery or torture was used until a confession was finally obtained. What was paramount in the minds of the Judges, Justices and others involved in the administration of Justice at the time, were the views clearly expressed by King James the First himself in his famous treatise 'Demonology', which became enshrined in the infamous Witchcraft Act of 1604.

James had spent a great amount of time and effort in the study of Witchcraft, and this had led him to an honest and sincere belief in the craft, as the opening passages of his work indicate:

> "The fear abounding at this time in this country, of those detestable slaves of the Devil, those witches or enchanters, hath moved me to despatch in post, this following Treatise of mine, not in any wise to serve for a show of my learning, but only to press thereby so far as I can, to resolve the doubting hearts of many, both that such assaults of Satan are most certainly practised, and that the instruments therefore merit most severely to be punished."

Close scrutiny of the evidence obtained at Examinations by the two magistrates Nowell and Bannister, reveal that many of what they considered to be 'voluntary confessions' were in keeping with what the King had written in his Treatise. This further adds weight to the assertion that the prosecution deliberately phrased questions at both Inquiry and Examinations which laid the accused open to admitting a certain pattern of criminal behaviour - the classic 'leading question'. In order to secure a safe conviction, it was necessary that the alleged offences were linked as closely as possible to the actual provisions of the 1604 Act. Today, most reasonable people would accept a confession as direct proof of the facts being confessed. However, there is always the danger in criminal cases that any confession may be misunderstood or used as a pretext for the omission to offer other equally valid and admissible proof of guilt. To this end, it is important in criminal evidence and procedure that no confession may be put in evidence, unless it is first established that it was offered, 'freely, without threat or inducement'. Even in such cases, the Court may exclude a confession from any evidence if it was made without a previous caution having been given to the accused, that they need not make a statement.

Trials are directed to prove facts by evidence and not by mere Inference or Surmission. Many legal problems arise with the testimony of accomplices, when it is in the interest of the alleged accomplice to throw blame on a co-defendant. Regarding the alleged 'confessions' obtained at the Witch Trials, there is no reliable information available that throws light on just how Nowell and Bannister obtained these confessions. In the absence of this, some doubts arise as to their legal validity or admissibility in Court. It can be only speculated that they may have resorted to the well-practised techniques in interrogation, of convincing the accused that their co-defendants had confessed to everything, thus providing sufficient information to convict them also.

This raises the question as to what extent Roger Nowell was personally involved in the initial Inquiries culminating in the Trials. James Crossley in his introduction to Pott's 'Discoverie', refers to Nowell as an 'eager and willing instrument in that wicked persecution which resulted in the Witch Trials of 1612'. He continues to describe how Nowell's 'ill-directed activities seem to have fanned the dormant embers into a blaze, and to have given aim and consistency to the whole scheme of oppression'.

Did Nowell really set out on a course of persecution - a literal 'witch hunt' in the Forest of Pendle, or was he simply responding to complaints submitted to him in the way that was expected from a local Justice of the Peace?

The Nowell family had lived in the area of Pendle Forest for generations and, as such, they would be familiar with the locals, their life styles and customs. Tales of superstitious happenings would have eventually filtered through to Read Hall, the home of

NOWELL OF READ

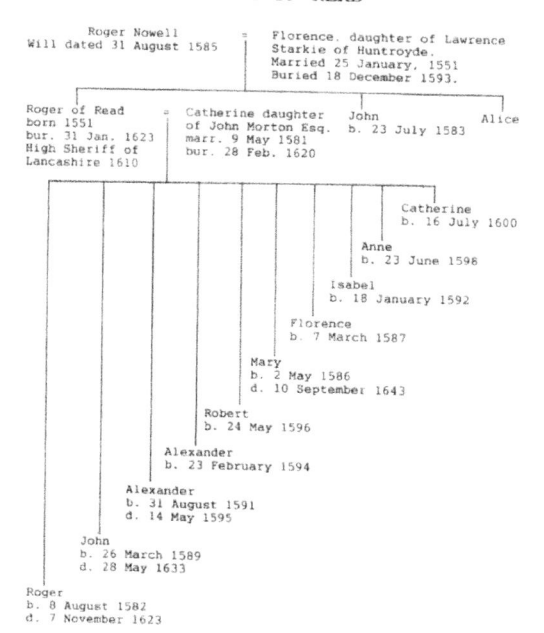

Roger Nowell = Florence, daughter of Lawrence
Will dated 31 August 1585   Starkie of Huntroyde.
                             Married 25 January, 1551
                             Buried 18 December 1593.

Roger of Read = Catherine daughter   John   Alice
born 1551   of John Morton Esq. b. 23 July 1583
bur. 31 Jan. 1623 marr. 9 May 1581
High Sheriff of   bur. 28 Feb. 1620
Lancashire 1610

Catherine
b. 16 July 1600

Anne
b. 23 June 1598

Isabel
b. 18 January 1592

Florence
b. 7 March 1587

Mary
b. 2 May 1586
d. 10 September 1643

Robert
b. 24 May 1596

Alexander
b. 23 February 1594

Alexander
b. 31 August 1591
d. 14 May 1595

John
b. 26 March 1589
d. 28 May 1633

Roger
b. 8 August 1582
d. 7 November 1623

the Nowell family. Nowell chose to put those initial rumours down to nothing more than idle gossip. However, once they had developed into serious accusations of criminal behaviour, he would have been obliged to take the necessary steps to investigate these claims.

From this view point, Crossley's comments of 'ill-directed activities' appears somewhat unfair and open to criticism. However, to ignore such Depositions and Informations would have rendered Nowell liable to removal from office for obstructing the course of justice. Once complaints had been acknowledged, he was obliged to set up an Inquiry and Examination which, once started, would inevitably set off a chain of events which could not be halted. In this sense, Nowell was caught up in the judicial web of legal procedure.

Why should such pitiful and inadequate people as the Pendle Witches cause so much fear and dread? Ronald Holmes makes a pertinent observation:

> "The common people really did believe that witches had the powers attributed to them, based on a simple cause and effect logic, no longer held except by the most primitive races. Religious history had turned the witch into a symbol of evil which was as powerful to the mind, in a negative way, as the symbol of the Cross is in a positive way."
> 'Witchcraft in British History' (1974).

The events of 1612 have an ironical twist to them in that, some twenty-one years later, the instrument of many convictions, namely Jennet Device, was herself returned to Lancaster to stand trial on a charge of Witchcraft. The felony of Witchcraft remained in force until the reign of George II, when an Act was passed in 1736 to repeal 'all previous Witchcraft Acts', [Appendix A]. Whilst it was no longer illegal to be a witch, it was not considered wise to profess such practices. To ensure that there was no return to the 'old practises', a further section was added to the 1736 Act which effectively controlled the dubious practices of fortune-telling and the like.

Europe soon followed Britain's example by repealing such of the Witchcraft Acts as were still in existence - France in 1745, Germany in 1775 and Spain in 1819. All references to 'Witchcraft' and allied practices were removed from the Statute Book and replaced by the Fraudulent Mediums Act of 1951 which was enacted essentially to control those who still carried out superstitious practices 'for gain' [Appendix B]. This Act is still in force at the time of writing.

The whole sad catalogue of events in 1612 can best be summarised by the inclusion of an extract from Edward Baine's famous *History of the County Palatine and Duchy of Lancaster* written in 1868. On the subject of Witchcraft in general, Lancashire in particular, and the role played by King James I, he states:

> "The sapient author (James) after having imagined a fictitious crime, placed the miserable and friendless objects of conviction, beyond all hope of Royal clemency. Having laboured to open the door for the most unjust convictions, the Royal fanatic adds that all witches ought to be put to death without distinction of age, sex or rank. This was the age of witchcraft and no county in the kingdom was more scandalised by the degrading and incredible superstitions than the County of Lancaster. In the present day when the term of 'Lancashire Witches' seems only to excite feelings of gaiety and admiration, it is not possible to conceive how different were the

sentiments which were produced by these magical words in the 17th century."

"Gentle reader, although the care of this Gentleman, the Author, was great to examine and publish this his work according to the Honourable testimony of the Judges, yet some faults are committed by me in the printing, and yet not many, being a work done in such great haste, at the end of a Term, which I pray you, with your favour to excuse."
Thomas Potts

A Prayer of Exorcism

"As it is said in the 17th Chapter of St. Matthew at the 20th verse: By (your) faith, ye may remove mountains, be it according to faith, if there is or ever shall be witchcraft or evil spirit that haunts or troubles this person or this place or this beast, I adjure thee to depart, without any disturbance, or molestation or trouble in the least; in the name of the Father, and of the Son, and of the Holy Ghost. Amen."

FINIS

APPENDICES

APPENDIX A

The Repeal of The Former Witchcraft Acts 1736

"Be it enacted by the King's Most Excellent Majesty, by and with the advice and consent of the Lords Spiritual and Temporal and the Commons in Parliament assembled, and the authority of the same as follows:-

No Prosecution, Suit or Proceeding shall be commenced or carried out against any person or persons for Witchcraft, Sorcery, for Inchantment or Conjuration, or for charging any of them with any such offence in any Court whatsoever in Great Britain.

And for the more effectual preventing and punishing any pretences to such arts and powers as are before mentioned, whereby ignorant persons are frequently deceived and defrauded, be it further enacted that if any person pretend to exercise or use any kind of Witchcraft, Sorcery, Inchantment or Conjuration, or undertake to tell fortunes or pretend from his or her skill or knowledge in any occult or crafty science to discover where or in what manner any Goods or Chattels supposed to have been stolen or lost may be found, every person so offending shall for every such offence suffer imprisonment by the space of one whole year."

[9 George II. 1736]

APPENDIX B

Fraudulent Mediums Act 1951

"Be it enacted by the King's Most Excellent Majesty, by and with the advice and consent of the Lords Spiritual and Temporal, and the Commons in Parliament assembled, and by the authority of the same, as follows:-

1. Any person who:
(a) With intent to deceive, purports to act as a Spiritualistic medium, or to exercise any powers of telepathy, clairvoyance or other similar powers or
(b) In purporting to act as a Spiritualistic medium or to exercise such powers as aforesaid, uses any fraudulent device, Shall be guilty of an offence.

2. A person shall not be convicted of an offence under the foregoing subsection unless it is proved that he acted for reward; and for the purposes of this section, a person shall be deemed to act for reward if any money is paid, or other valuable given in respect of what he does, whether to him or any other person.

3. A person guilty of an offence under this section shall be liable on summary conviction to a fine not exceeding the statutory maximum (£2,000), or to a term of imprisonment for a term not exceeding two years or to both.

4. No proceedings for an offence under this section shall be brought in England and Wales except or with the consent of the Director of Public Prosecutions.
[14 & 15 George VI. c 33].

SELECTED BIBLIOGRAPHY

Ainsworth, W. H., *The Lancashire Witches*, 1848.
Baines, E., *History of the County Palatine and Duchy of Lancaster*, 2 Vols., 1868.
Harland, J., A Lancashire Charm in Cypher against Witchcraft and Evil Spirits, in *Transactions of the Historical Society of Lancashire and Cheshire*. Vol 4., 1851.
Holmes, R., *Witchcraft in British History*, 1974.
Hughes, P., *Witchcraft*, 1952.
Parrinder, G., *Witchcraft*, 1958.
Weeks, W., John Webster: Author of the Display of Supposed Witchcraft, in *Transactions of Lancashire & Cheshire Antiquarian Society*, Vol 39. 1921.
Whittaker, T.D., *History of Whalley,* 1818.
Wilkinson, T.T., Popular Customs and Superstitions of Lancashire, in *Transactions of the Historical Society of Lancashire and Cheshire*, Vol 13., 1860.

Printed in Great Britain
by Amazon